W9-BEB-333

# Monkeys Are a Lot Like Us

## By Allan Fowler

**Consultants**

Robert L. Hillerich, Professor Emeritus,
Bowling Green State University, Bowling Green, Ohio;
Consultant, Pinellas County Schools, Florida

Lynne Kepler, Educational Consultant

Fay Robinson, Child Development Specialist

SCHOLASTIC INC.
New York  Toronto  London  Auckland  Sydney
Mexico City  New Delhi  Hong Kong

Design by Herman Adler Design Group
Photo Research by Feldman & Associates, Inc.

ISBN 0-516-23804-3

12  11  10  9                                    4  5  6/0

Printed in the U.S.A.

First Scholastic printing, March 2001

Is it a monkey or is it an ape?

This capuchin has a tail,
so it must be a monkey.

Most monkeys have tails,
but you will never see an
ape with a tail.

Monkeys are much smaller than apes, too. The pygmy marmoset is the smallest monkey of them all.

Monkeys that live in the forests of South America and Central America are called New World monkeys.

They spend almost all of their time in trees.

If you could hear this
howler monkey howling,
you'd know how it got
its name.

With its long, skinny
arms and legs, the spider
monkey may remind you
of a spider.

It uses its long tail to swing from tree to tree. Many New World monkeys can do this.

They can also use their tails to pick things up.

But not the Old World monkeys of Africa and Asia. They can't use their tails the way New World monkeys can.

Old World monkeys live
on the ground as well
as in trees. And many
of them are bigger than
New World monkeys.

Baboons are big and fierce
and travel in troops.

# Mandrills are the largest monkeys.

You can easily tell whether
a mandrill is male or
female by its coloring.
If it has patches of bright
red and blue, it's a male.

The plainer looking
mandrills are females.

Proboscis means nose.
So you can see why
this monkey is called
a proboscis monkey.

Rhesus monkeys are often seen in zoos. They belong to a family of Old World monkeys called macaques.

# Monkeys are like people in some ways.

They live in families or
groups of families. One
monkey may act as leader.

The mothers take good care of their babies. They nurse them and teach them things.

Some monkeys are so smart that they figure out how to use sticks as tools. Monkeys have hands with five fingers.

But only Old World monkeys
have thumbs like humans.
Their thumbs make it easy
for them to grasp objects.

They can clean each
other's fur . . .

# peel fruit . . .

and pick up their food
when they eat.

When they do things like that, monkeys may remind you of people.

Monkeys are fun to watch, whether they seem to be acting like people . . .
or are just going about their monkey business.

# Words You Know

## New World Monkeys

capuchin

howler monkey

pygmy marmoset

spider monkey

# Old World Monkeys

baboon

mandrill

proboscis monkey

rhesus monkey

# Index

## About the Author

Allan Fowler is a free-lance writer with a background in advertising.
Born in New York, he lives in Chicago now and enjoys traveling.

## Photo Credits